resilience

For my parents, Linda and Robert, whose support has made it possible to live the life of my dreams.

Published in 2023 by Welbeck
An imprint of Welbeck Non-Fiction Limited
part of Welbeck Publishing Group
Offices in: London – 20 Mortimer Street, London W1T 3JW & Sydney – Level 17, 207 Kent St, Sydney NSW 2000 Australia
www.welbeckpublishing.com

Text © Welbeck 2023
Design and layout © Welbeck Non-fiction Limited 2023

ISBN 978-1-80279-597-4

Printed in China

10 9 8 7 6 5 4 3 2 1

resilience

10 WAYS TO RECOVER FROM BURNOUT AND EXHAUSTION

JOLINDA JOHNSON

WELBECK

contents

what's your why?

1

"I rise. I rise. I rise."

"Three times?"

"Yep, three times."

Sitting in meditation earlier that morning, I had a vision of those lines tattooed across my left arm. Several hours later, I was sitting in the waiting room of my favourite tattoo studio here in Barcelona, waiting to get inked.

Being that it was our thirteenth time working together, my tattoo artist was used to me coming to him with ideas that had some kind of deeper meaning. I couldn't just get something permanently drawn on my body because it looked pretty. Whatever beauty it bestowed also had to come with some teeth.

"So, you have to tell me. What's this one about?"

"Resilience. And Maya Angelou. Have you ever heard of her poem, 'Still I Rise?'"

"Not sure that I have, but I feel like I'm about to."

As he prepared the tattoo stencil and got the table set up, I read it to him out loud. By the time I had finished, he was convinced that I needed those three lines on my arm as well:

I rise. I rise. I rise.

i rise.
i rise.
i rise.

there's
no need to
rise if you've
never been
knocked
down

When I think about resilience, I can't help but think of the sentiment behind those words. Perhaps like you, I've had to be resourceful, push through my limitations and come out the other side time and time again. Being a single mother in a foreign country while running your own international coaching business tends to have that effect.

According to the American Psychological Association, resilience is "the process and outcome of successfully adapting to difficult or challenging life experiences and flexibility and adjustment to external and internal demands". If you're anything like me, you've got a whole long list of competing demands that you wake up to every morning and go to sleep with every night. If you're also a high achiever, you know what it's like to measure yourself against those demands and the pressure that comes from constantly trying to meet them.

If we have the resources to meet those challenges head-on, we come out the other side stronger than we were before. Resilience, after all, comes as the result of doing hard things. There's no need to rise if you've never been knocked down. Unfortunately, when it comes to navigating life's difficulties, many of us lack the necessary tools to make it through the storms. Instead of tending to our nervous systems and caring for our bodies and minds, we reach for cheap substitutes that only mask the discomfort and the pain. We constantly throw ourselves into choppy waters, hoping we won't drown, while at the same time forgetting that we never learned how to swim.

stress is inevitable.
burnout is optional.
resilience is possible.

This book was written from a desire to help you build resilience against the chronic stress and burnout that have become hallmarks of the twenty-first century.

As a result of reading through the following pages, you'll learn practical ways to regulate your nervous system, lower your stress levels and reconnect your body and mind. You'll also walk away with a better understanding of what burnout is and the many ways your body tries to warn you when it's on the way so you can course correct before you crash. My hope is that the exercises you find here will eventually become a regular part of your everyday life. As someone who has experienced burnout and recovered from it twice, I can tell you that prevention is a whole lot easier than the cure.

what's your why?

Before you continue, take a moment to think about an intention you have for reading this book. What's your "why" for wanting to reduce your current levels of stress and become more resilient against burnout? It might be as simple as a single word or something more concrete like a specific goal. Share it here in the lines below and come back to it as you move through the chapters that follow.

My intention for reading this book is . . .

....

....

....

....

....

....

....

....

....

....

....

chronic stress without recovery

2

Since I started my business back in 2016, all of my clients have needed help building resilience against burnout and recovering from years of chronic stress. As high achievers, they've worn "busy" like a badge of honour and used "stressed" as a measure of success. After all, if you're out in the world doing big things, stress is an unavoidable part of life, right?

Truth be told, not all stress is bad. In fact, good stress (the kind that gets your heart racing and your hormones surging as a result of something exciting) even has a name: eustress. Acute stress (the kind that you feel when you're speaking in public, taking an exam or working against a tight deadline) also has its place as it can improve cognitive function and keep you hyperfocused on the task at hand. As long as you have sufficient time to recover, acute stress can definitely have some benefits.

Notice how I said *as long as you have sufficient time to recover.* This is where most of us get ourselves into trouble. Instead of giving our bodies the opportunity to return to baseline, we rush off to the next big thing. We start pushing down on the gas pedal (also known as the sympathetic nervous system) right when we should be stepping on the brakes. To understand this concept better, let's take a quick look at what's actually happening in the body when you're under stress.

not all stress is bad

stress response: first wave

In the first wave of the stress response, your amygdala (also known as the "survival brain") perceives a threat through your senses.

This triggers the endocrine system (your hormones and the glands that secrete them) to release adrenaline. This initial adrenaline rush helps to push blood into your muscles, releases glucose (sugar) into the bloodstream and dilates the bronchial tubes in your lungs for better breathing. In a matter of seconds, everything is being diverted to support energy and brain focus. On the flip side, anything that's not going to help you fight against the incoming threat (or run away from it) gets dialled down. This includes eating food, fighting infection and making babies. Now is not the time for your digestive, immune or reproductive systems to shine.

stress response: second wave

In the second wave of the stress response, the amygdala and Hypothalamic-Pituitary-Adrenal (HPA) axis work together to adjust your stress levels accordingly. This is when you decide to fight, flee or freeze. In the fight scenario, you're moving towards the stressor. In the flight scenario, you're moving away from the stressor and in the freeze scenario, you're playing dead. Centuries ago you might have had occasion to fight against a lion, run away from a tiger or play dead in the face of a bear. These days, however, you could find yourself getting involved in an argument, running away from a difficult conversation or freezing up in front of an upsetting text.

While the amygdala determines the best response, the HPA axis activates the main stress hormone cortisol to boost immune function and replenish the energy stores that became depleted during the adrenaline rush of the first wave.

Once the perceived threat has passed (that unexpected email, the surprise visit from your ex, the presentation only you could deliver) your body begins returning to baseline.

As I mentioned earlier, the sympathetic nervous system is like the gas pedal, but now it's time to pump on the brakes. Also known as "rest and digest" or "feed and breed", the parasympathetic nervous system helps everything come back online, including everything that was deprioritized as a result of acute stress. But here's where most of us get stuck: until the survival brain is allowed to fully recover, the

stress response:

recovery

sympathetic nervous system remains activated and the stress response will keep getting triggered. Put it another way, if you continue to be stuck in a stress activating situation, you'll become stuck in the stress response. Welcome to chronic stress!

When it comes to chronic stress, you're asking yourself to rev up again when you haven't even begun to come down. What's more, your ability to tolerate stress lessens every time you override your body's signals to slow down. Eventually this can lead to epigenetic changes (how your genes work) that result in chronic inflammation. We don't need to get into the chronic stress won't just last for a few moments, it can go on for years specifics of inflammation, but you should know that chronic inflammation can lead to chronic pain, chronic fatigue, fibromyalgia, migraines, arthritis, eczema, cardiovascular disease and irritable bowel syndrome (IBS), to name a few. Unlike acute stress, chronic stress won't just last for a few moments, it can go on for years.

total body dysregulation

You may think of burnout as just another form of exhaustion, but the final stage is a state of total body dysregulation. Does that sound heavy? It is.

The first day I met my friend Michael Stephens, founder and CEO of We Create Space, a global retreat and workshop planning service, the topic of burnout came up. As we began to compare notes about our lived experiences, I was struck by all of the similarities.

"So, one day, I woke up and I couldn't move my neck. Like at all!"

"Whaaat? You've got to be kidding me! That's what happened to me too."

As strange as it sounds, in the summer of 2011 I woke one morning totally unable to move my neck. Literally overnight it had become an immobile block of cement. First came the rigidity, then came the pain and I ended up in my doctor's office by the end of the following day.

She was just as confused as I was and decided that it would be best for me to see a traumatologist, even though I hadn't been in any kind of accident. In the days leading up to my visit with him, I started doing some research and stumbled upon a chronic condition called ankylosing spondylitis (AS). When I brought it up with the traumatologist, he said I should spend more time reading romance novels and less time reading articles about spinal arthritis. He sent me home that day with a neck brace, a painkiller and a reminder not to take the word of misogynistic doctors. Eventually, I found an osteopath who took me seriously and referred me to his friend, who was a rheumatologist. After several tests to confirm it, I was officially diagnosed with ankylosing spondylitis in 2012.

Because of the way chronic stress impacts the body, burnout can indeed result in a health condition that you have to manage for life. I now see the direct correlation between my autoimmune disease and my many years of unmanaged stress, as well as all of the ways I abused my body in an attempt to "handle it". I sometimes wonder if things might have turned

24

out differently, had I known earlier about the practices that I'll be sharing with you later in this book. The reality is, we often have plenty of time to do things differently if we're ready and willing to heed the warning signs.

burnout can result in a health condition that you have to manage for life

HORMONES 101

Throughout this book, you'll see me refer briefly to a number of hormones that get thrown off as a result of chronic stress. If you're not sure what they are, here's a basic review that can help:

Insulin: A hormone released by the pancreas that causes cells to absorb glucose (sugar) from the blood and take it to the liver, muscles and fat tissue. As a result of chronic stress, your body can become less sensitive to insulin, ultimately leading to insulin resistance and diabetes.

Cortisol: The main stress hormone, it's produced in the adrenal glands that sit on top of the kidneys and can become high, dysregulated and ultimately low as a result of chronic stress. Chronically elevated cortisol can lead to insulin resistance, and insulin resistance in turn can lead to chronically elevated cortisol.

Oestrogen: The primary female sex hormone, although it is present in biologically male bodies as well. Throughout the reproductive years, it dominates the first half of the menstrual cycle and is responsible for building up the lining of the uterus. In times of stress, oestrogen and progesterone can become imbalanced, resulting in worse symptoms of premenstrual syndrome (PMS) and heavier periods.

Progesterone: A hormone produced as a result of ovulation when it is released by a temporary endocrine gland in the ovaries called the corpus luteum. In times of stress, the body favours production of cortisol over progesterone. Since progesterone receptors regulate oestrogen, too, little progesterone results in relative oestrogen dominance. In biologically male bodies, it's produced in the adrenal glands and testes and is a precursor to the primary male sex hormone testosterone.

Testosterone: The primary male sex hormone produced in the testes, although it is also produced in the ovaries and adrenal glands in biologically female bodies. Testosterone can also be converted to oestrogen. Chronic stress and lack of sleep can cause low testosterone levels, and low testosterone levels can in turn induce feelings of anxiety, lack of motivation, fatigue and decreased strength and muscle mass.

Thyroid: The hormone necessary for controlling metabolism, produced in the thyroid gland. About 80 per cent of thyroid hormone is an inactive form (T4, thyroxine) and 20 per cent is an active form (T3, triiodothyronine) that can be used by the cells. Chronic stress can cause the thyroid gland to become underactive (such is the case with Hashimoto's hypothyroidism) or overactive (Graves' disease).

the warning signs of burnout

3

the warning signs of burnout

When you're experiencing acute stress, the body shifts all of its energy to dealing with the immediate threat while diverting energy away from everything else. When we stay in the stress response, the body continues to prioritize the production of stress hormones above all else.

In her book, *Brilliant Burnout*, Nisha Jackson PhD, describes four stages of adrenal fatigue: "wired and tired", "stressed and depressed", "burnout resistance" and "burnout". This inspired me to create what I call the Four Phases of Burnout, highlighting both the physical symptoms that you're likely to experience as well as the behaviour modifications that you'll probably use to cope. Here's what that looks like in real life:

the four phases of burnout

when your head hits the pillow, your mind is still on overdrive

PHASE ONE

- You're feeling stressed, but your body can still produce significant amounts of the stress hormone cortisol to help you meet those demands head on.

- You're likely to feel hypervigilant and can easily focus on the tasks of the day, possibly even volunteering to take on more.

- Unfortunately, when it's time for bed you often find it hard to unwind and while your body is tired when your head hits the pillow, your mind is still on overdrive.

- You may have trouble falling asleep, while others may struggle to stay asleep. Waking up between the hours of 1 and 3 a.m. could become a nightly occurrence.

- You'll likely to start turning to stress reaction cycle habits (e.g. overdoing it on sugar and alcohol) in an attempt to soothe yourself.

PHASE TWO

- If the stress continues and you haven't given your body any time to rest and reset, your adrenal glands, thyroid, ovaries and nervous system continue the struggle to keep up as best they can.

- You'll notice a feeling of tiredness throughout the day or a reliance on that second cup of coffee to keep you going in the afternoon.

- You can still get things done, but you may find yourself plagued by indecision, forgetfulness, lack

sleep becomes

more problematic

of focus and a persistent feeling that you're off your game. Hello, brain fog!

- Sleep also becomes more problematic at this stage as you tend to feel awake right at the time you most want to fall asleep.

- If you menstruate, you'll probably notice an uptick in your symptoms of premenstrual syndrome (PMS)/ premenstrual tension (PMT), as well as heavier periods.

PHASE THREE

- Your nervous system, adrenals and brain are doing their best to support you, but that means sex hormones like testosterone, progesterone and oestrogen are becoming unstable.

- In terms of energy, you're dragging throughout the day (especially in the morning) and are beginning to feel run down.

- Because stress also affects digestion and gut health, you may also be experiencing food sensitivities, irritable bowel syndrome (IBS) and/or constipation and dealing with skin complaints like acne, dandruff and eczema.

- You'll likely swing between extreme procrastination and extreme overwork. You put things off because you're tired, but then have to hustle hard to get everything finished at the last minute.

- If you menstruate, you can expect symptoms of oestrogen dominance to start cropping up, including a sharp increase in your PMS/PMT symptoms, a decrease in your sex drive and other issues that can't be so easily ignored, including fibroids, ovarian cysts and cystic breasts.

PHASE FOUR

- You are officially exhausted, even after a full night's sleep. In the previous stages, your body was doing its best to keep up with your increased demand for stress hormones, but that's not happening anymore either. At this point, cortisol takes a nosedive and your edge is long gone.

- Slower thyroid function shows up as a slowed metabolism, dry skin, constipation, trouble sleeping and weight gain.

- The energy you do have will be devoted to handling less important, immediate tasks as you lack energy and vision for long-term goals.

- At this point, all systems of your body, including the thyroid, skin, lungs, heart, joints, adrenals, immune system, stomach, pancreas and liver are being affected.

- The end result could be a chronic condition such as an autoimmune disease.

Although it may feel like you go from being at the top of your game to not being able to get out of bed overnight, these changes are often years in the making. Even if you find yourself in the final phase, there is always the possibility to do things differently and show up for yourself in ways you never had before.

three types of burnout

Many people think burnout is always the result of being overworked: too much to do in too little time. While the root cause is chronic stress without recovery, the way we experience that doesn't always look the same. It might surprise you that people can also become burnt out from having to do too little or not really knowing what they're meant to be doing at all.

OVERLOAD

With this type of burnout, you're stretched way too thin. It might be due to your own ambition and desire for success, or it could be the result of having an excessive amount of responsibility or circumstances forced on you beyond your control. Either way, it leaves you feeling depleted with little chance to catch your breath. One of the biggest misconceptions about burnout is that having a love for what you do acts as some kind of protection, but it can actually make it harder to recognize when your body needs a much-needed break.

Motto for this group: Can't stop, won't stop.

motto for this group: can't stop, won't stop

UNDERCHALLENGED

With this type of burnout, your stress doesn't come from having too much to do, but rather having too little. For someone who always has a lot going on, having too little to do might sound like the very opposite of a stressful situation, but being under-challenged leaves much to be desired. Imagine having to show up to a situation every day and feeling bored out of your mind, understimulated beyond belief and unrecognized for everything you could contribute if only you were given the chance. As a result, you find yourself becoming increasingly frustrated at the lack of opportunities for professional development and growth.

Motto for this group: Same sh*t, different day.

NEGLECT

With this type of burnout, you feel helpless and hopeless. You have little or no say-so in your day-to-day, so you constantly feel like things are out of your control. Roles at work are ill-defined and the likelihood that you'll be blamed for overstepping (or slacking off) is high. As you can imagine, always trying to guess what you should be doing in the absence of clear expectations can take its toll and eventually you stop trying to exert any kind of agency or decision-making power at all.

Motto for this group: Grin and bear it.

A FEW THINGS TO KEEP IN MIND:

1   Burnout is more than just being tired of your job.

2   Burnout consists of four distinct phases that involve the brain (central nervous system), the autonomic nervous system (sympathetic and parasympathetic nervous systems) and the endocrine system (hormones and glands).

3   Burnout is the result of chronic stress without recovery.

4   People who do what they love can, and often do, burn out.

5   Your level of success does not determine your likelihood for burnout; your ability to manage your stress and recover from it effectively does.

Now that you have a better understanding of what burnout is, the impact that it has on your body and the different ways that it can show up in your life, let's start exploring the different ways that you can start building your resilience.

QUESTIONS FOR REFLECTION

1 When you think of your personal and professional life, what is most likely to trigger your stress response?

....

....

2 When is the last time you remember feeling stressed out? What did your mind have to say about it? What did you notice happening in your body?

....

....

3 How has burnout shown up in your life thus far? What symptoms from the above lists do you notice in yourself now or in the past?

....

....

4 What's one new thing you learned in this chapter that you can share with a friend?

....

....

how has burnout shown up in your life?

nutrition

4

"You're going to give yourself diabetes."

It was the spring of 2010 and I had just had a difficult conversation with my mom about my weight. Since arriving in Barcelona to start a new teaching job six months earlier, I had put on no fewer than 50 pounds. If you've ever been to Barcelona, you'll know that finding delicious food is never a problem. You can't walk a city block without passing by a restaurant or café that seems to be calling your name. Unfortunately, my ever-increasing waistline was not a result of sampling all the local fare.

Unlike now when I actually take pleasure in my food, back in those days eating was just another way to escape from my stress. I was away from my family and friends, starting my life from zero in a foreign country, feeling totally lost in my early twenties and working excessively hard at a job that I didn't really enjoy. If you recall the descriptions of the three types of burnout from Chapter One (page 38), it was a combination of overload (having too much to do) and neglect (not having much direction when it came to doing it). On that particular day, I had just confessed to finishing off an entire box of biscuits and a jar of chocolate hazelnut spread sitting alone in my room on a Sunday afternoon. This was not a one-off occurrence, but something that had become part of my regular weekend routine. Everything I was doing to calm the emotional stress of my mind was creating an incredible amount of physical stress in my body and it was definitely starting to show.

eating was just another way to escape stress

You're probably familiar with emotional stress, but you might not know too much about physical stress. You can think of emotional stress as happening in your mind, while physical stress happens in the body. Some examples of emotional stress include feeling irritated or overreactive with your loved ones, ruminating over a negative point of view, feeling anxious and easily overwhelmed. Some examples of physical stress include changes to your energy levels, headaches, gas and bloating, trouble sleeping and muscle pain. Unfortunately, the things that many of us use in an attempt to dial down our emotional stress are the very same things that turn up our physical stress:

emotional stress

vs physical stress

- Alcohol may help you relax in the moment, but has been shown to interrupt sleep patterns and trigger anxiety the next day.

- Working your way through a box of cookies might give you a sweet release, but unstable blood sugar contributes to mood swings, sadness and irritability in the hours that follow.

- Coffee gives you the illusion of energy, but also puts added strain on your already overworked adrenal glands, especially when you're reaching for that second or third cup of the day.

DRINK UP!

Did you know that even being mildly dehydrated is a form of physical stress? Just being 500 ml short of the recommended daily intake of water can cause your cortisol levels to rise. When it comes to staying hydrated, aim for 2.75 litres a day, 500 ml of which can come from water-rich fruits and vegetables.

Try having 1 litre of water first thing in the morning, 1 litre mid-morning after breakfast and another mid-afternoon after lunch. After dinner, you can switch to herbal tea, which counts towards your daily water intake too.

If the idea of sipping plain water gives you a case of the blahs, here's a simple way to zhuzh things up with a delicious water infusion:

6 cups (1.5 litres) water

1 medium cucumber, sliced

2 limes (1 juiced, 1 sliced)

Handful of spearmint leaves cut into ribbons

try to have one litre of water first thing in the morning

Combine all the ingredients in a jug and leave in the fridge for a few hours before drinking.

Limes help beat bloat, improve digestion and reduce inflammation. The silica and antioxidants in the cucumber give your skin a healthy glow, while spearmint has compounds that promote relaxation and reduce stress.

protein + fat + fibre

If you want to support your body through times of stress, it's key to keep your blood sugar balanced. So what's the easiest way to do this? Include protein, fat and fibre in all of your meals and snacks.

Think of protein, fat and fibre as the magic trifecta that will keep your mood steady and your energy strong. This is because of the stabilizing effect it has on blood sugar and therefore insulin. If you recall from the last chapter, insulin is a hormone released by the pancreas and it tends to get thrown off when cortisol (the main stress hormone) is high (see also page 28).

When you eat too much sugar, like I was doing by eating rows of cookies in one sitting, it creates fluctuations in your blood sugar. Insulin is like the bodyguard that's meant to keep all of this under control, so the more sugar you eat, the more insulin the pancreas releases. If you continue overdoing it, though, your insulin levels remain chronically high. The cells eventually stop responding to it as they should, which is what happens in the case of insulin resistance.

Under normal circumstances, cortisol counterbalances insulin, but in times of chronic stress, chronically high levels of cortisol can lead to insulin resistance and insulin resistance can lead to chronically high levels of cortisol. As tempting as it can be to reach for the chocolate bar or bag of crisps, you're really just giving your body more work to deal with as it's desperately trying to come back to balance. Aiming to include a combination of protein, fat and fibre in your meals and snacks can make all the difference.

protein

It's important to get enough protein every day, but especially during times of chronic stress. Unfortunately, it's also the macronutrient that the majority of my clients skimp on the most. As a general rule, aim for 1 to 1.5 g of protein per 2.2 pounds of body weight or a serving the size of your palm at each of your meals.

In addition to keeping blood sugar stable, eating enough protein can also contribute to a better mood, higher levels of concentration and fewer sugar cravings. Some excellent sources of protein include:

- **Fish** (especially oily fish like wild, responsibly caught salmon, mackerel and sardines)

- **Organic or free-range poultry** (chicken, turkey)

- **Grass-fed lean beef**

- **Legumes** (like lentils and chickpeas)

- **Tofu and tempeh** (fermented soy)

- **Protein powder** (preferably organic grass-fed whey or plant-based with no artificial sweeteners)

include protein, fat and fibre in all of your meals

OVERNIGHT OATS WITH PROTEIN POWDER

SERVES 1

Most people know about adding a scoop of protein powder to their favourite smoothie, but I also love to have it in my overnight oats. Here's the combination that I have for breakfast most days of the week:

½ cup (75 g) rolled/old-fashioned oats

¼ cup (30 g) grass-fed chocolate whey protein powder

½ teaspoon Ceylon cinnamon (optional, but great for blood sugar balance)

1 cup (200–250 ml) unsweetened almond milk

1 large spoonful nut butter

Raw cacao nibs

Add the oats, protein powder and cinnamon to a large jar and stir together. Pour in the almond milk, stir well and place in the fridge overnight. In the morning, transfer to a bowl, top with nut butter and sprinkle with cacao nibs.

fat

There are a lot of things I miss about the nineties, but the fat-free craze is definitely not one of them! Along with fibre, fat slows down digestion and the rise of glucose (sugar) in the bloodstream. This means that insulin doesn't spike, you're more likely to feel satisfied after a meal and remain full for hours to come.

Some of the best sources of fat include:

• **Extra virgin olive oil**

• **Extra virgin coconut oil**

• **Grass-fed butter**

• **Nuts and seeds**

• **Ghee**

You can also eat more oily fish, which is rich in omega-3 fatty acids, or consider taking an omega-3 supplement. Omega-3 fatty acids affect physical and perceived emotional stress by directly influencing the brain and central nervous system cells. They can reduce perceived distress symptoms, prevent aggression towards others during times of stress and diminish the negative health consequences that come from chronic stress exposure.

fat slows digestion

benefits
include
reduced pain
and inflammation,
better memory
and brain
function and
a boost
in mood

GOLDEN MILK

SERVES 1

The golden colour of this drink comes from turmeric, a powerful anti-inflammatory herb that's excellent for counteracting physical stress. Besides tasting delicious, some of the benefits include reduced pain and inflammation, better memory and brain function, and a boost in mood when consumed regularly. If you struggle with constipation in the morning, having 1-2 teaspoons of ghee can encourage more regular to eliminations. The fat from the ghee also helps your body better absorb the nutrients from the turmeric and can also lowes inflammation, especially in the gut.

1 cup (250 ml) unsweetened almond milk

1 teaspoon ghee

½ teaspoon Ceylon cinnamon

½ teaspoon ground ginger

2 teaspoons ground turmeric

A pinch of black pepper

1-2 teaspoons honey to taste

Warm up the almond milk and the ghee in a saucepan until simmering, then blend in the spices and honey.

fibre

One of the best ways to include the recommended 35–45 g of fibre in your daily diet is by including carbs. Although low-carb diets have attracted a lot of attention in recent years, taking your carb intake too low isn't the best idea either, especially when you're already stressed. High-fibre carbs can help you sleep better, stay regular and feel calmer throughout the day. Some of my favourites include:

sleep better and

feel calmer

- **Fruits:** berries, avocados, apples, kiwis, prunes

- **Vegetables:** broccoli, carrots, spinach, kale, artichokes, sweet potatoes

- **Legumes:** lentils, chickpeas, kidney beans, split peas

- **Whole grains:** oatmeal, buckwheat, brown rice, popcorn

- **Nuts and seeds:** almonds, chia seeds, flax seeds.

Aim for four to six cups of vegetables a day and two to three servings of fruit.

IN THE MOOD TO MUNCH?

Sometimes you just feel like snacking, but it's oh too easy to overdo it on processed junk. The next time you're in the mood to munch, satisfy yourself with one of these high-fibre snacks instead:

- **Popcorn popped on the stove with extra virgin coconut oil**. I add lots of Himalayan pink salt and drizzle with flaxseed oil. Popcorn is a high-fibre snack, great for keeping you regular and feeling full. Coconut oil and flaxseed oil both help to support your hormones and gut and Himalayan pink salt is just what your adrenal glands ordered.

- **Dark chocolate squares (85/90 per cent cocoa) and a side of apple slices.** If you crave chocolate, it could be that your body is looking for a hit of magnesium (or maybe you just need a moment of pleasure). Either way, dark chocolate will give you a dose of both. When you combine chocolate and apples, you not only get the extra fibre, but the specific antioxidants present in both complement each other and become even more effective.

- **Brown rice cakes with tahini and nori seaweed.** In addition to providing the fat in this snack, tahini (sesame seed paste) has compounds that may protect brain health. Seaweed adds a bit of extra flavour and the iodine supports the production of thyroid hormone. The brown rice cake adds crunch and is a gluten-free source of fibre.

satisfy yourself with one of these high-fibre snacks

- **Carrot sticks with guacamole.** Not only do carrots give you that satisfying crunch, they're also high in fibre and antioxidants such as vitamin A and beta-carotene. Interestingly, they've been found to prevent the reabsorption of oestrogen back into the intestine, making them an excellent choice for anyone interested in preventing the relative oestrogen dominance that can come with periods of prolonged stress. Pair carrot sticks with guacamole for a well-rounded snack.

putting it all together

Here are some examples of what including protein, fat and fibre in all your meals and snacks would look like on a typical day.

If you include meat and fish in your diet, your day could look like this ...

- **Breakfast:** a smoothie with protein powder, avocado and berries

- **Morning snack:** an apple and a handful of almonds

- **Lunch:** a big salad with lots of veggies, fish and olive oil

- **Afternoon snack:** a couple of kiwis and a pot of plain yogurt

- **Dinner:** free-range chicken with broccoli and roasted sweet potatoes.

If you're a vegetarian or vegan, your day could look like this ...

- **Breakfast:** a smoothie with plant-based protein powder, avocado and berries

- **Morning snack:** an apple and a handful of almonds

- **Lunch:** a big salad with lots of veggies, beans and olive oil for lunch

- **Afternoon snack:** carrot sticks and hummus

- **Dinner:** lentil curry with brown rice and coconut milk.

Healthy eating isn't about following the perfect diet. It is, however, about supporting your body with foods that make you feel even more alive.

healthy eating isn't about following the perfect diet

QUESTIONS FOR REFLECTION

1 What time of day do your cravings usually hit?
  What do you typically reach for?

....

....

2 When you do indulge, are you relishing in the
  present moment or trying to escape from it?

....

....

3 How might your regular food choices be affected
  by your sleep (or lack thereof)?

....

....

4 What supportive foods are you currently including
  in your regular routine? Which ones would you like
  to eat more of?

....

....

exercise

5

excuse me, i'm not sure where to start. it's my first time here.

**"Excuse me. Sorry, I'm not sure where to start.
It's my first time here."**

I had just arrived at a place I never thought I'd set
foot in: my local gym. I had gone with the idea that
I would do the elliptical (cross trainer) machine or
the treadmill for half an hour and instead had ended
up in a strength training class called Body Pump.
Despite feeling nervous, I walked up to the instructor,
who I have to admit was my primary motivation for
joining that day, and did something that was very
out of character for me: admitted that I had no idea
what I was doing. Fortunately, he was not only good-
looking, but also incredibly kind as he showed me
the equipment and made sure that I was comfortable
with everything before we began.

When I was a girl, I was constantly teased for my lack
of athletic ability and for many years I was hesitant
about exercising in public, even as an adult. If I did
work out, it was usually out of fear of gaining weight
or as a punishment for what I had eaten the day
before. All of that changed, however, in the autumn
of 2016. On the brink of separating from my then-
husband and unsure of what life would be like as a
single mum, I found myself facing a kind of stress I
had never experienced before. On the Holmes-Rahe
Stress Inventory scale, divorce rates number two in
the top ten most stressful life events, just after the
death of a spouse or child and just before marital
separation. I knew that I didn't want to lose myself in

destructive habits like I had in my first year in Spain, so this time I was determined to take a different tack.

I completed the class that day without any additional weights, just the bar itself to concentrate on my form. From the beginning, everyone made me feel welcome and that gave me the little push I needed to keep coming back. Over the next few weeks, I continued adding more and more weight and pushing myself through every set. If I could finish comfortably, I knew I wasn't doing enough and that I was actually stronger than I had originally thought.

It wasn't long before I realized what a boon my regular gym classes were for my mental health. Eventually, I added Zumba and Body Balance to the mix. On the days when I woke up feeling sad and overwhelmed from the heaviness of divorce proceedings, working out gave me a chance to come back into my body and seek refuge from the storm. I started to see that the stronger I was physically, the more I could handle emotionally. My body was no longer my adversary, but instead my greatest ally.

When you're feeling overstretched by your responsibilities and everything seems to be coming at you all at once, it can be tempting to live from the neck up and ignore your body's needs. As I discovered in the year surrounding my divorce, however, engaging in regular exercise is key to reducing the negative impact of chronic stress. There are many different ways that you can move your body to bring it back to safety and let it know that the imminent threat has passed. As Emily Nagoski, PhD, and Amelia Nagoski, DMA, assert in their book, *Burnout,* "physical activity is the single most efficient strategy for completing the stress response cycle." All movement has value, but the point is to find something that you actually enjoy doing so that it becomes something you look forward to instead of something you dread.

the stronger i was physically, the more i could handle emotionally

SO, YOU SAY YOU DON'T LIKE EXERCISE?

If exercise isn't included on your list of favourite things, here are four ideas that can help:

1 Decide that you love your body as it is.

That may sound counterintuitive, but as the famous Carl Rogers' quote goes, "when I accept myself just as I am, then I can change." When you no longer work out in the hope of losing weight or transforming your physique, you'll no longer be tied to the results. This means that you can be fully present in the experience without being weighed down by expectations and the disappointment of not having them fulfilled.

2 Don't let your fear of what other people think determine your actions.

For years, I was afraid of not doing everything "just right", of not being the best from the beginning, of other people's judgement and ridicule. The fact is that no one could have been as hard on me as I was on myself and at the end of the day a person who criticizes you is really just making up for their own insecurities.

3 Pair it with pleasure.

When trying to get into a new habit, it always helps to pair it with something that brings you joy. Maybe that means buying a new pair of trainers in a colour that feels happy and fun. Perhaps it's investing in a new set of athletic gear that you can look forward to putting on or even creating a playlist with all the songs you love to groove to – even when I'm feeling sad, music always gets me going!

4 Get accountability and support.

It's a lot easier to show up to the gym when you know someone is expecting you. Nowadays I prefer to work out at home, but when I was first building the habit of regular exercise into my routine, I was fortunate enough to have a trainer who made everyone feel like they mattered. I also made a number of "gym buddies" that I looked forward to seeing before or after class. Never underestimate the power of connection.

cardiovascular training

Cardiovascular training, or "cardio" for short, is an effective way to care for your heart, increase longevity and manage stress. According to the American Heart Association, you should aim to perform moderate-intensity cardiovascular activity for a minimum of 30 minutes five days per week, or vigorous-intensity cardiovascular activity for 20 minutes three days per week.

increase longevity

and manage stress

Moderate-intensity activities have you at 55 to 70 per cent of your maximum heart rate with an effort that makes your breathing heavy. You can still talk, but holding a conversation becomes more difficult. Vigorous-intensity cardiovascular activities exert you even further to the point where you can only speak a few words, or at times barely breathe.

If you're just starting out, you might opt for low intensity continuous cardio, also known as "steady state", since your heart rate remains in the same range. Since the intensity is lower, the optimal amount of time you spend doing this kind of activity is usually longer. For example, a moderate-intensity activity might look like a 30-minute jog whereas a low-intensity activity could be a 60-minute walk.

Cardiovascular training reduces feelings of depression and anxiety while increasing the levels of endorphins in the brain. Endorphins are neurotransmitters, or chemical messengers, produced in the hypothalamus and the pituitary gland. They're often referred to as "feel-good" chemicals because of the positive effect they have on a person's mood. They've also been shown to increase confidence, leading to a more positive self-image as well as higher self-esteem.

Some examples of cardio include:

- **Brisk walking**

- **Jogging**

- **Rowing**

- **Hiking**

- **Using the elliptical (cross trainer) machine**

- **Cycling**

- **Water aerobics**

- **Swimming**

positive
self-
image
and
higher
self-
esteem

strength training

You might think that strength training is only good for building muscle or "bulking up", but the benefits go way beyond the appearance of your physique.

Like aerobic exercise, it can also help to improve your mood as well as your memory and learning performance due to something called muscle-brain crosstalk. For those who menstruate, it also helps to reduce the symptoms of premenstrual syndrome/premenstrual tension (PMS/PMT) due to its positive effect on relative oestrogen dominance.

In times of chronic stress, the body dials down the production of progesterone in favour of creating more of the main stress hormone cortisol (*see also page 28*). Since progesterone is meant to modulate oestrogen, this often results in a relative oestrogen dominance and a higher accumulation of fat. As fat cells also secrete oestrogen and higher oestrogen levels encourage the production of fat, building more lean muscle through strength training can bring things back into balance and counteract this effect. Additionally, if you're experiencing symptoms of low testosterone like fatigue, low sex drive and lack of motivation, strength training is the best form of exercise to get your levels back up.

If you're new to strength training, start with lighter weights and gradually build up. Keep in mind that you should feel the first signs of muscle fatigue, commonly referred to as "the burn", about 75 per cent through the set. If you plan on working out at home, it's a good idea to have a set of light, medium and heavy dumbbells as different muscle groups will require different weights. In general, you want to aim for five to ten exercises targeting the major muscle groups for two to four sets of ten to 15 repetitions. That can be as low as six if using a heavy weight. The heavier the weight, the lower the repetition.

A basic full-body routine might consist of bicep curls, tricep extensions, shoulder presses, squats and walking lunges doing three rounds of ten reps of each exercise. Rest for 30 seconds between each exercise and 90 seconds between rounds.

hiit

High Intensity Interval Training (HIIT) involves alternating periods of work and periods of rest, or active recovery. It's been found to decrease anxiety, stress and depression as well as increase resilience.

decrease anxiety, stress and depression as well as increase resilience

Like the moderate-intensity cardiovascular training described above, it will also give you that hit of endorphins that you've been looking for. It's not recommended to do this kind of exercise every day, but two to three times a week can usually be tolerated well without greater risk of injury. It can be performed at the end of a strength training session or scheduled as an independent workout.

Tabata is one HIIT protocol that's gained popularity in recent years and consists of 20 seconds of working at your maximum effort, followed by ten seconds of rest for eight rounds, for a total of four minutes. Whenever you are doing this kind of training, make sure to include five to ten minutes of moderate-intensity cardio to warm up and then finish with a five-minute cool down. If you'd like to give it a try, there are many workouts available online that include four rounds of Tabata that can be completed in 20 minutes.

One caveat: because HIIT has also been shown to increase levels of circulating cortisol, this isn't the best choice for those who are already in the later stages of burnout and should be avoided by everyone late in the day or too close to bedtime.

SMALL, BUT CONSISTENT

If you think that exercise has to take up a lot of time to be effective, you might be avoiding it because you think you can't carve out an hour or two from your busy day. Fortunately, this isn't necessary when it comes to effectively managing stress, enhancing your mental focus or improving your overall health.

Shorter workouts are also great for helping you get into the habit of regular exercise. It can feel a lot less threatening to the emotional brain to think of jumping around on a trampoline for ten minutes as opposed to attending an hour-long boot-camp class. Here are some ideas to get you started:

- **Ten minutes of yoga**

- **Seven-minute circuits where you do a series of different exercises for 60 seconds each**

- **Ten minutes bouncing on a rebounder (mini-trampoline)**

- **Ten minutes of dancing**

- **Twenty to 30 minutes of strength training**

get into the habit of regular exercise

A lot of my clients have been conditioned to think that if it's not high-impact, it's not worth doing. However, overdoing it when it comes to high-intensity training can lead to elevated cortisol levels, thyroid dysfunction and sleep disturbances. Keep in mind that if you're feeling more depleted than energized after your workout, lower the intensity and give your body the time it needs to recover.

body, breath and mind

qigong (chee-gong)

There are over 3,600 different styles of Qigong (Chee-gong), but all of them focus on three core elements: body, breath and mind. The specific movements of Qigong help to re-energize the body by promoting the flow of blood and oxygen, sharpen the mind by improving mental clarity and focus, and harness the power of the breath to calm the sympathetic nervous system and come back to a state of balance.

If you're recovering from burnout or just don't feel like a high-intensity workout first thing in the morning, Qigong could be just right for you.

yoga

Among yoga's many benefits, regulation of the nervous system is at the top of the list. Various studies have demonstrated that practicing yoga regularly can help improve sleep, mood, concentration and overall well-being. Depending on how you choose to practice, it can incorporate breathing, meditation and mobility, all of which activate the parasympathetic nervous system in their own unique ways.

If you've ever felt intimidated by yoga because you lack flexibility, you'll be happy to know that yoga isn't about who can bend the farthest. In fact, the whole point is to meet your body where it's at and tend to it accordingly. Some poses that can be particularly restorative in times of stress include cat-cow, child's pose, legs-up-the-wall pose and savasana (corpse) pose.

Stretching and mobility exercises in general can help relieve stiffness and improve circulation.

relieve stiffness and

improve circulation

shaking

Shaking is one of the simplest ways to activate the parasympathetic nervous system and get you out of the fight-or-flight response.

Begin by shaking your right arm, then shake your right leg. Now shake your left arm, followed by your left leg. Finish by shaking your body from head to toe. Continue for five minutes or more and notice the difference in how you feel. Give yourself the opportunity to really let go and allow your body be your guide.

allow your body to be your guide

QUESTIONS FOR REFLECTION

1 Think of a time when your body felt energized and alive. What were you doing?

....

....

....

2 What kind of exercise could you start doing that would involve an element of that experience?

....

....

....

3 What's one negative belief you have about exercise that's been holding you back?

....

....

4 What would change for you if you were to release that belief? Now think of something positive and affirming that you could replace it with.

....

....

....

sleep and rest

6

"It's nine o'clock. You should already be in bed."

"It's time for YOU to be in bed, Mama. You need to sleep too."

This is a typical exchange between my eight-year-old son and me on any given night. Since he doesn't have to get up until 8 in the morning, going to bed at 9 p.m. still gives him the solid 11 hours that are recommended for school-aged children. If he had his way, however, we would both go to bed at the same time.

I honestly can't remember a point in my life when I ever looked forward to going to bed. I've always preferred to stay up late. Like many of us who have little ones, it can often feel like the only time we get to kick back and relax is in the wee hours of the night.

When cortisol and melatonin are within their optimal ranges, feeling tired by 10 p.m. should be a given. Unfortunately, high cortisol levels due to chronic stress can give you a second wind right when you would otherwise be tucking yourself in. If you've had time for yourself and feel like you've accomplished everything on your to-do list, it can be easier to power down and call it a day. On the other hand, if you've been up to your eyeballs in responsibility or too tired to get everything done, you might feel tempted to stay awake. Succumb to this temptation enough nights in a row and going to sleep past midnight could easily become your new normal.

power down and call it a day

As early as nine o'clock sounds, especially for an adult who's been living in Spain for the last 14 years, my son does have a point. With the exception of the summer months, it's already dark outside, which is one of the most basic signals that affects your circadian rhythm.

Circadian rhythms, as defined by the National Institute of General Medical Sciences, are "physical, mental, and behavioural changes that follow a 24-hour cycle". When your hormones are working optimally and your stress levels are under control, a typical circadian rhythm involves being awake during the day and asleep for eight hours or more at night.

physical, mental and

behavioural changes

Within a part of your brain called the hypothalamus, there is a group of 20,000 nerve cells that form the suprachiasmatic nucleus (SCN). The SCN signals to the pineal gland when it needs to produce melatonin, largely as a result of your exposure to light and dark.

You can therefore do a lot to support your circadian rhythm by exposing yourself to sunlight first thing in the morning and dimming all of the lights before bed. Staying up late to scroll through Instagram on your phone, however, will have the opposite effect.

not enough sleep has been linked to high blood pressure, irregular menstrual cycles, hypothyroidism, depression and anxiety

sleep is critical for hormonal balance and cell repair

It's not just melatonin that gets thrown off when you don't practice good sleep hygiene. Many other hormones are also affected by the duration and the quality of your sleep each night:

Insulin: Insulin sensitivity decreases and blood sugar remains high.

Cortisol: Production of cortisol increases.

Leptin: Production of leptin (the satiety hormone) decreases.

Ghrelin: Production of ghrelin (the hunger hormone) increases.

Thyroid: Production of Thyroid Stimulating Hormone (TSH) increases.

Growth hormone: Production is suppressed.

Progesterone, oestrogen, and testosterone: All decrease over time.

CORTISOL AND MELATONIN

Cortisol may be the main stress hormone, but it has a number of functions even when all is going well, including getting you out of bed in the morning. It follows what's known as a diurnal pattern:

- Between 6 and 8 a.m. you get a burst of cortisol (the cortisol awakening response) that gets you out of bed

- Thirty minutes after waking up from a good night's sleep, cortisol levels are at the highest they'll be all day

- Following the morning peak, cortisol levels then fall to less than half that level by noon

- Cortisol levels reach the lowest point around midnight, which then allows your cells to repair and heal.

As mentioned above, melatonin is a hormone produced in the pineal gland of the brain and high levels let your body know when it's time to go to sleep. It has an inverse relationship with cortisol, so when cortisol is high, melatonin is low. This is good at 8 a.m. when you need to start the day, but is less than desirable past 10 p.m. when you ought to be winding down.

When cortisol becomes dysregulated as the result of chronic stress, production of melatonin can also be suppressed. This often leads to getting a "second wind" when you should be getting ready for bed and a feeling of tiredness upon waking in the morning.

Our libido also takes a direct hit. Besides the toll that a lack of sleep takes on your sex hormones, like oestrogen and testosterone, in favour of your stress hormones, like cortisol, you are less likely to be in the mood for love if you are exhausted. This may seem basic but being too tired is the most common reason most couples lose interest in having sex, at least according to sex therapists.

Just as sleep can affect your hormones, hormones can also affect your sleep. Ask anyone in perimenopause (the ten or so years leading up to the final menstrual period) and they'll most likely tell you that their sleep has been off. Low progesterone, for example, can lead to waking up in the middle of the night while low oestrogen may result in night sweats that require a full change of your sheets.

chronic stress can affect your sleep and lack of sleep can make you chronically stressed

If you've been following along this discussion, you should know by now that with chronic stress comes raised levels of cortisol. Since cortisol and melatonin have an inverse relationship, high cortisol at night results in low melatonin levels when it should actually be the other way around. This dysregulation typically results in the classic "wired but tired" feeling. Even when you don't have any physical energy left, you could easily stay awake bingeing on a true crime documentary or getting lost in a social media vortex. Add a sugary treat and you've just added elevated blood sugar to the mix. You might be safe and sound in your comfortable home, but your body is in a state of physical stress, unable to tend to the daily tasks of regeneration and repair that can only happen in the deeper stages of the sleep cycle.

A recent study found that those who stayed up past midnight had a higher risk of cardiovascular disease and this statistic was even higher for women. It's also been suggested that depressive episodes and suicidal thoughts are likely to be more prevalent when sleep is disturbed. When you don't get the recommended seven to nine hours of shuteye, or when your sleep is continually interrupted, physical and emotional stress is the inevitable result. Here are just a few ways that skimping on sleep stresses your body out:

- **Memory loss and trouble concentrating**

- **Changes in mood and behaviour**

- **Weight gain**

- **High blood pressure**

- **Weakened immunity**

- **Increased risk of diabetes and heart disease.**

Poor-quality sleep and chronic stress go hand in hand, so it only makes sense that improving the quality of your sleep will also increase your resilience. Here are a few ideas to get you started:

- Go to bed and wake up at the same time every day. In terms of our hormones, they respond best to a regular routine, so make sure to be consistent with your bedtime, even on the weekends.

poor-quality sleep and chronic stress go hand in hand

- Sleep in total darkness. No night lights, no light streaming in through your bedroom blinds, just darkness. Not sleeping in the dark interferes with the production of melatonin, optimal levels of which help us to fall asleep.

- Get enough sunlight. The more natural light your body receives during the day, the more likely it will be to stay in tune with regular day-night rhythms. Always aim to get sunshine in the morning if you can.

- Disconnect from electronic devices an hour before bed. If I had to choose one tip that has made the biggest difference in my own life, this would be it! The electromagnetic frequency can prevent the brain from moving through the five cycles of sleep correctly. Plus, the blue light from mobile phones and tablets can actually trick the brain into thinking it's still daytime.

- Just say no to alcohol and caffeine. If you have to have one last coffee, make sure it's before 2 p.m. In terms of alcohol, it may seem like the perfect sleep aid but the truth is that it keeps you from entering the phases of deep, restorative sleep that you need throughout the night.

- Exercise daily (just not right before bed). Exercise in the morning or midday is a great way to get a better night's sleep, but working out too close to your bedtime can release the stress hormones cortisol and adrenaline and prevent you from falling asleep when you need to.

- Create a calming bedtime routine. Even if mobile phones didn't emit blue light and electromagnetic waves, they are a constant source of stimulation and excitement. Instead of spending your last waking hour scrolling through social media or cuddling up with a livestream, take some time to disconnect, read a book, have a relaxing bath or journal about the day. Establishing a bedtime routine is key.

FATIGUE EATING

Have you ever noticed that when you don't get enough sleep you feel like eating more than usual? That's because without sleep, ghrelin (aka the "give me food and give it to me now" hormone) goes up and leptin (aka the "hold up, that's enough food for now" hormone) goes down. Lack of sleep also makes you more likely to choose foods high in sugar, refined carbohydrates and caffeine. All of these give you a quick energy rush at first, but leave you feeling even more drained in the end.

On days when you're dragging, reach for foods rich in protein to keep your blood sugar stable, starting with breakfast. A protein-based smoothie, a veggie omelette or a bowl of yogurt with ground flax and berries will get you a lot further than cereal and coffee ever will.

Drink extra water and try to get outside in the afternoon when you're most likely to experience the biggest energy dip.

When you get home, make a concerted effort to disconnect from your laptop and phone – the artificial light can make it harder to get a good night's sleep, no matter how much your body needs it.

taking things slow

One of the hardest lessons I've had to learn is how to slow down. We hear over and over again how important it is to rest, but rest can only be restorative if you're willing to release the guilt: the guilt for not working to your full capacity, the guilt for not being a reliable resource, the guilt for doing less than this, that or the other person expects you to do.

You might have spent years pushing yourself into overdrive by overcommitting, keeping busy and stretching yourself thin until there's nothing left to give. And if you can't do it all, your inner critic convinces you that you must be failing so you work harder still to prove that you can succeed. In a world that celebrates constant output, it's no wonder success has become synonymous with exhaustion while rest has become something to fear. Rest can therefore be a radical act of resilience and self-care.

My own relationship with rest has largely changed as a result of living in a country that appreciates a slower pace. When I first arrived in Spain in 2008, I asked myself multiple times a day why things couldn't be faster and more efficient. Why did my favourite stores have to close in the middle of the day? Why couldn't I go to the supermarket on Sunday? Why were people just strolling around the streets instead of walking with purpose and direction? After a while I

rest can be a radical act of resilience and self-care

started asking myself why I was in such a rush. Wasn't the entire point of life to enjoy the journey anyway? Eventually I began to shift my perspective and found my overall stress levels start to come down as a result.

the power of rest

If you're like many of my clients, you might be wondering exactly what rest is and how you can possibly incorporate it into your high-paced lifestyle. Dr Saundra Dalton-Smith talks about seven different kinds of rest including physical (both passive and active), mental, spiritual, emotional, social, sensory and creative. Dalton-Smith contends that you can get adequate amounts of sleep, but without the opportunity for rest, you'll "still be waking up tired."

Here's what these seven types of rest currently look like in my life:

Physical (passive): Stretching out on my sofa in the middle of the afternoon when the sun is pouring in through the window, closing my eyes and cuddling my two dogs as I drift in and out of sleep.

Physical (active): Keeping a regular bi-weekly appointment with my massage therapist.

Mental: Writing down anything that might still be swirling around in my mind before I go to bed.

Spiritual: Spending time every morning at my altar in meditation and prayer.

Emotional: Meeting with my coach and having a space where I can be vulnerable as a leader.

Social: Prioritizing time with a few very special friends whose energy makes me feel replenished every single time.

Sensory: Putting my phone on airplane mode or simply leaving it at home when I go out for a walk.

Creative: Having fresh flowers and beautiful artwork in my home; going to the beach at sunset and watching the moon rise.

Resting is far from doing nothing, but it can feel confronting to take time out for yourself. This is why it's essential to affirm your worth independent of your productivity. You are worthy simply for being, independent of what you are doing. No matter what, rest isn't something you earn for a job well done, but rather something that you must give yourself as a basic human need.

you are
worthy
simply
for
being

QUESTIONS FOR REFLECTION

1 At 10 p.m., what are you most likely to be doing? Is this helpful or harmful when it comes to getting a good night's sleep?

....

....

....

....

2 On a scale from 0–10, how hard is it for you to step away from your phone at the end of the day? What's something that might motivate you to power down an hour earlier?

....

....

....

....

3 What's one thing that you could do this week that would improve the quality of your sleep?

....

....

....

....

meditation
and
breathwork

7

you need to start meditating

"You need to start meditating."

The first time someone ever told me this, I was in the eighth grade sitting across from my father at the kitchen table. I had come downstairs to have breakfast before school and he was already reading the paper and drinking his coffee. He asked me if I was ready for my upcoming mathematics exam and I confessed that I was a bit nervous because maths was never a subject that came easily to me.

After giving me his usual lecture about how I needed to focus, he followed that with the suggestion that I try meditation. He said it would help me feel less nervous and give me the clarity and peace of mind I needed to discover whatever answers I might need. Intrigued, I finished my bowl of cereal and tried closing my eyes. I probably made it to a full five minutes; maybe two.

I would love to say that meditating every morning for the final months of junior high led to a lifelong practice, but like most things your parents introduce you to during those teenage years, I rejected it as something obligatory, unnecessary and uncool. I spent the next 20 years reading articles about meditation and even purchased several books, but despite learning about its many benefits, I never managed to fit it into my daily routine. Something always stopped me from making the time and space to just be still. I was afraid to let go, afraid of the blank slate, afraid of trying to slow down my ever-racing mind. I was also terrified of being alone with my body, just me, myself and I. What if I couldn't stop thinking? What if I was no good at quieting my mind?

If you've ever let these or similar fears stop you from meditating, I'm happy to share some very good news: the goal of meditation isn't to clear your mind, it is to simply be present. If you've ever judged yourself for not creating the proverbial blank slate, you can let that idea go. The more you meditate, the more you're able to move through life with mindfulness and ease because you realize that, just like your thoughts, everything is just passing through.

meditation benefits

Every time you meditate, you're eliciting the body's relaxation response and thus reducing the activity of the sympathetic nervous system. If you recall from earlier in the book, your sympathetic nervous system is like the gas pedal of a car, revving you up to either fight against the stressor or flee from it as fast as you can. This means that people who meditate regularly experience the benefits of a more regulated nervous system including:

move through life with mindfulness and ease

- Lowered blood pressure

- Improved blood circulation

- Lower resting heart rate

- Slower respiratory rate

- Less anxiety

- Lower blood cortisol levels

- More feelings of well-being

- Less stress

- Deeper relaxation

- Increased creativity.

A FEW THINGS THAT HAPPEN WHEN YOU DON'T MEDITATE

As much as I love reaping the benefits of a regular meditation practice, I'm also motivated by my desire to avoid the consequences of not having one. Here are a few things that start to happen when I don't make meditation a daily priority:

A louder inner critic: When your stress response is activated, you become hypervigilant to anything that looks wrong, including everything you don't like about yourself. If you find that you're camped out in front of your mirror picking at your pores instead of sitting down at your computer banging out your latest project, unprocessed stress could be to blame – the same stress that meditation is so good at eliminating.

No inner compass: Another great thing about meditation is that it gets you in touch with your core (the essence of who you are, not the six-pack you've been hiding away). When you intentionally carve out 15 to 30 minutes every morning to just be with yourself, connect with your body and sit with your soul, you go into each day feeling solid. You're also a lot more likely to live in reality and not just your false perception of it.

Less feeling, more hiding: By meditating, you give yourself the time and space you need to simply be with your feelings without any expectation of changing them. Especially in times of stress or unexpected change, it's easy to look to other people to make everything better and cure all the wounds yet the ultimate responsibility always falls on you. Sitting in meditation gives you a chance to meet yourself with kindness, compassion and care.

Easy buttons galore: Easy buttons are those things that give us the illusion of stress relief, but actually make our lives more difficult in the long run. There are a lot of easy buttons and you can actually press more than one at the same time: eating cookies with a bottle of champagne while scrolling through social media with Netflix playing in the background (for example,...).

your mind will be clear, open and creative

Another beautiful bonus when it comes to regular meditation is that it creates brain cohesion, which means there's greater communication between the left side and the right side of the brain. As a result, you're going to find that your mind is able to remain clear, open and capable of coming up with creative solutions even when you are in the face of a lot of different demands.

In only two months, meditation can change the brain enough to be visibly detectable by MRI, shrinking the fear centre and enlarging the centres responsible for creative problem-solving, not to mention happiness and love. Interestingly, it's not just for dealing with the stress we're experiencing in the here and now either. The unprocessed stress we experienced years ago can also be diminished when we meditate. If you weren't able to meet your feelings and process them appropriately from experiences like getting a divorce, losing your job, or that last time you moved into a new apartment, chances are that stress is still hanging around. Meditation gives it a chance to finally be released. There are literally thousands of ways to meditate, but here are three of my personal favourites.

MINDFULNESS MEDITATION

Sometimes you just need to sit with your feelings. After spending time on my meditation cushion, focusing on my breath and checking in with my body, I'm able to face myself and whatever emotions I'm carrying with greater ease.

• Sit comfortably, either cross-legged on the floor or on a meditation cushion. If you prefer to be on a regular chair that supports your back but allows your head to move, that's also an option.

you need to sit

with your feelings

- Now close your eyes and bring some awareness to your breath. You don't need to control anything here, so just continue to breathe naturally.

- Notice how the body moves with each inhalation and exhalation. Observe your chest, shoulders, ribcage and belly

- If your mind wanders, return your focus back to your breath.

- Stay like this for two to five minutes to start, working your way up to 15 to 30 minutes every day.

walking meditation is perfect for when you have a million things swirling around in your head and you just need a break

WALKING MEDITATION

Also known as "mindful walking", walking meditation is perfect for when you have a million things swirling around in your head and you just need a break from #allthethoughtsintheworld. It's been shown to reduce physical stress and improve overall mood. As you can guess from the name, it's all about bringing conscious awareness to your surroundings, whether surrounded by nature or in the hustle and bustle of a city street.

- Before you set out on your walk, set the intention to remain present.

- As you move along, try to go at a slower pace than usual and actually savour the sights, sounds, smells and sensations around you. Feel the way your feet hit the ground, the breeze on your cheek, the blood pulsing through your fingertips.

- Keep an eye out for anything particularly pleasant or positive, pausing for a moment to acknowledge each one in your mind, making sure that it's registering in your conscious awareness.

- Take in the kindness and care that you're showing towards yourself in that moment of just letting yourself be and as always, remember to breathe! See also Breathwork, page 129.

MUSIC MEDITATION

Some argue that meditation should be done in silence or with nothing more than ambient noise. If you can't "just be" with your thoughts, the answer isn't to tune up your favourite playlist, rather to meet yourself in this discomfort. While it might not be ideal, music can make sitting in stillness feel a lot less threatening and acts as a gateway to the mindfulness meditation practice described above for those who are just starting out.

- When choosing which music to listen to, instrumental tracks or those specifically designed for meditation tend to work best. You might also find that certain sounds in nature like ocean waves or birdsong help you to relax.

- Sit comfortably, either cross-legged on the floor or on a meditation cushion. If you prefer to be on a regular chair that supports your back but allows your head to move, that's also an option.

- Close your eyes and begin directing your full attention to the music. The idea is to be fully present with the sounds that you hear.

- If your mind wanders, return your focus to the music and the feelings that it's eliciting in your body.

- Stay like this until the track comes to an end. It can be helpful for this reason to choose something that lasts the same amount of time as you intend to meditate.

breathwork

When I work with my clients, we always start off in the same way: by taking a few minutes to just breathe. It always amazes me that for most of the brilliant beings I work with, it's the only time in their day that they've devoted to slowing down and getting in touch with their bodies.

When you practice deep breathing, a number of incredible things happen:

- It anchors you into the present moment, helping to relieve feelings of anxiety and depression.

- It switches on your parasympathetic nervous system, which lets you know that it's safe to relax.

- It helps the body release toxins and improves the digestion and assimilation of food.

- It improves blood quality, releasing carbon dioxide and increasing oxygen supply.

- It helps you become more resilient to stress and encourages energy to move more freely. This will also encourage you to move more freely through life as well.

With each breath of air, you take in oxygen and release the waste product carbon dioxide. Since breathing is so automatic, you probably don't stop to think about how these two gases are flowing in and out of your body. However, poor breathing habits alone can contribute to anxiety, panic attacks, depression, muscle tension, headaches and fatigue. That's independent of anything else happening in your life! By learning to breathe correctly, you can more easily calm the mind, relax the body and have more energy to fully participate in your day.

When we breathe, we typically use one of two patterns. The first is chest, or thoracic, breathing and, unfortunately, it actually promotes stress. The second is abdominal, or diaphragmatic breathing, which is deeper and slower than shallow chest breathing, as well as more rhythmic and relaxing. The diaphragm is a muscle that sits just below the lungs, separating the chest from the abdomen. It's the primary muscle involved in respiration, contracting every time you inhale and relaxing every time you exhale. Although the diaphragm is working to help you breathe all day long, practicing diaphragmatic breathing, as you'll learn below, can strengthen this muscle and help it to function more efficiently.

One of the best things about breathing is that you can literally do it anytime, anywhere. I'll share with you some of my favourite techniques below, but if you're ever in doubt, you can experience a positive difference simply by slowing things down. Nervous before giving a big presentation? Slow down your breathing. Feeling frustrated as you wait in line at the supermarket? Slow down your breathing. Already overwhelmed and then one more thing gets added to your to-do list?

SLOW. DOWN. YOUR. BREATHING.

DEEP BELLY BREATHING

Also known as diaphragmatic breathing, deep belly breathing is a simple and effective way to get yourself out of the stress response.

1 Start by sitting down with both feet on the floor, or lying down on your back if that feels more comfortable.

2 Place one hand on your chest and the other on your belly.

3 As you inhale, feel your belly expand and your hand begin to rise. The hand placed over your chest should remain relatively still.

4 As you exhale, press gently on your abdomen and feel the release as your belly goes down.

5 Repeat this for two to three minutes, or however long you need.

hold your breath a moment before you exhale

BREATHING WITH AN AFFIRMATION

This is a simple variation of the deep belly breathing practice described above. You can replace the word "relax" with anything that resonates with you in the moment. For example, "release", "let go", "be calm", "be present", "surrender".

1   Take a deep breath in and feel your belly start to rise as you say to yourself, "May I ..."

2   Now hold your breath a moment before you exhale.

3   Exhale slowly and deeply through pursed lips as you say to yourself, "Relax."

4   As you take your next deep breath in, notice where there is any tension in your body or where you are experiencing resistance. Every time you breathe out, Imagine that the tension is leaving your body as well.

5   Repeat this cycle for two to three minutes, or however long you desire.

BOX BREATHING

One of my favourite breathing techniques is called box breathing. Practicing box breathing will get you out of fight-or-flight mode and essentially resets your breath while helping the body and mind to settle down.

1   Sit with your back against a chair and your feet on the floor. Close your eyes.

2   Begin to slowly exhale for four seconds. Hold your breath while slowly counting to four.

totally disconnect

as you breathe

3 Breathe in through the nose while counting slowly to four. Hold your breath while slowly counting to four.

4 Exhale through the mouth once more. Hold your breath while slowly counting to four.

5 Repeat this cycle four times.

As you carry out this exercise, imagine tracing the sides of a square to give you a visual cue or download one of the many apps available to keep track of the time so you can totally disconnect as you breathe.

ALTERNATE NOSTRIL BREATHING (NADI SHODHANA PRANAYAMA)

Also known as Nadi Shodhana Pranayama in Sanskrit, alternate nostril breathing can be done on its own or in addition to your meditation practice. Roughly translating to "subtle energy clearing breathing technique", it's excellent for relieving stress and bringing the energy system of the body back into balance. Begin with five cycles and then slowly work up to as many as 25.

1   Sit in a comfortable position, either in a chair or cross-legged on the floor.

2   Place the index and middle finger of your right hand on your forehead.

3   Close your right nostril with your right thumb. Inhale through the left nostril.

4   Exhale through the left nostril. Close your left nostril with your ring finger and open your right nostril.

5   Inhale through the right nostril. Exhale through your right nostril.

6   Close your right nostril with your thumb. Inhale
    through the left nostril, beginning the next cycle.

One simple rule: You will always switch after every
exhalation. Whichever nostril you inhale through, you
exhale through.

LAUGHTER

Are you surprised to see laughter listed as a breathing
exercise? In addition to releasing feel-good endorphins
and reducing the stress hormone cortisol, laughing
also helps to oxygenate the blood. Every time you
laugh, you're giving your lungs a chance to squeeze
out stale air and take in more fresh oxygen. See what
happens when you give the following exercise a try.

1   Start in a seated position with your hands resting at
    your sides.

2   Bring a smile to your face, signalling to your brain
    that something pleasant is about to happen.

3   Now raise your hands up above your head and start
    to giggle.

4   As you begin to lower your hands, stretching them
    out towards each side, say "Weeeeeeee!" By the
    time you get halfway down, you should be in the
    midst of laughter.

QUESTIONS FOR REFLECTION

1 How do you feel about starting a regular meditation practice? What benefit motivates you the most?

....

....

2 What would most likely get in the way of you meditating? What would be your go-to excuse?

....

....

3 Where do you plan to meditate? What can you include in this space to make it even more inviting?

....

....

4 Of all the breathwork practices described above, which appeals to you most and which could you try this week?

....

....

bring the energy system of the body back into balance

mindset
shifts

8

you come from a long line of persevering women. we don't quit.

"I don't know if I can go through with this."

"What do you mean? You've come so far, you can't stop now."

In the spring of 2020, I was in the middle of planning a launch for a new 12-month program called Thrive. I was working with someone at the time who told me the best way to fill it with my ideal clients was to run a five-day challenge. There I was, at the beginning of the pandemic, a single mother in lockdown with my six-year-old son, planning to run an original week-long course, along with a Facebook group entirely for free. The night before it was supposed to start, I could literally feel myself jumping out of my skin.

If my body could talk, it would be saying, "Woah, slow down. You've got a lot on your plate right now. Maybe you should call off the challenge and give yourself an extra week. Maybe two." My thinking brain, however, told me quite a different tale. It went something like: "You've come so far, don't give up now. Everyone's looking forward to doing the challenge, you don't want to let them down. You come from a long line of persevering women. We don't quit."

As you can see, the thinking brain doesn't acknowledge the difficulty of the situation that you're in. It also doesn't care about what your body is trying to say. At best, it will emphasize your ability to overcome any challenge. More than likely, however, it will just make you feel afraid, judged and incapable of making the decision that actually prioritizes your needs. It could sound like the voice of your mother, your father, your ninth grade algebra teacher or a combination of various authority figures that have influenced you over the years.

In the end, I went through with the challenge and nearly made myself sick in the attempt. When I had finished delivering everything to a group that I had built up to over 400 people, not one person signed up. From that day forward, I promised myself that I would never sacrifice my health and happiness for a business commitment again. No matter what the thinking brain had to say about it, I knew that there had to be another way.

thinking brain override

In her book, *Widen the Window*, Elizabeth A. Stanley, PhD, introduces the concept of "thinking brain override". Thinking brain override happens when you ignore your body's needs and limits by suppressing your emotions and physical sensations. It relies heavily on personal and societal narratives that help you to essentially "override" your body's signals. While it helps you adapt in the short term, it eventually disconnects you from your inner wisdom, or what you "feel" to be true.

THREE WAYS CHRONIC STRESS IS BAD FOR YOUR BRAIN

Even though it can feel like your brain is on overdrive, the effects of chronic stress will eventually take their toll.

- **Chronic stress** causes the brain to shrink, specifically the prefrontal cortex. This is the area involved in decision making, judgement and our ability to concentrate.

- **Chronic stress** leads to fewer new brain cells being made in the hippocampus, which might make it harder for you to learn and remember things.

- **Chronic stress** also results in the loss of synaptic connections between neurons and puts you at greater risk of depression and Alzheimer's later in life.

When it comes to brain health, both exercise and meditation are your stress-busting buddies. They've both been shown to increase the hippocampus, which is just one of the areas that comes under attack. Meditation also thickens your prefrontal cortex, prevents further shrinkage and improves its connection with the amygdala so you can go through the day with a greater sense of calm.

fixed mindset + obsessive passion = fast track to burnout

If you want to put yourself on the fast track to burnout, try adopting a fixed mindset and mix that with an obsessive passion. A fixed mindset emphasizes limiting beliefs which ultimately discourage you from learning new talents and skills. It can look like this:

- **Believing there's only one job for you and no matter what, you have to make it work**

- **Viewing failure as a limit of your abilities**

- **Taking feedback and criticism personally.**

Obsessive passion blurs the lines that once separated you and your work until your whole life revolves around your career. It can look like this:

- **Having a strong urge to work on your business 24/7**

- **Feeling emotionally dependent on your work**

- **Having difficulty imagining life without your work.**

Not surprisingly, a fixed mindset combined with an obsessive passion is associated with declining physical health, a decreased attention span and higher levels of anxiety and stress. One of the most important shifts you can make, therefore, is choosing to adopt a growth mindset. A growth mindset emphasizes your ability to learn new talents and skills through effort and perseverance. With a growth mindset, you learn to accept that change is part of life and that there will always be more opportunities for success if your current pursuit doesn't pan out. It can look like this:

- **Openness to feedback**

- **Ability to admit and learn from mistakes**

- **Willingness to try new ideas.**

Because there's a much stronger emphasis on learning, trial and error is not only expected, but encouraged.

If you choose to go one step further and harmonize your passion (e.g. recognize when work is taking over your life and set boundaries accordingly) you'll experience a greater sense of well-being, better work-life balance and more sustainable achievement. When a growth mindset is paired with harmonious passion, work becomes a part of your life instead of your entire life. When your entire sense of self doesn't rest on your performance on the job, you're more likely to slow down when necessary, heed your body's signals and get off the train before reaching burnout as your final stop.

breaking up with perfectionism

When you embrace perfectionism, you abandon yourself. By constantly chasing after a standard which doesn't exist, you disconnect yourself from the human experience in the here and now. Afraid of what would happen if you stood out, you hide away whatever doesn't fit in, shielding the world from your differences rather than acknowledging them as gifts. Feelings are suppressed. Beauty is ignored. Talents go unshared. And this has serious consequences that most people fail to realize, or at least fail to mention:

- You don't use your voice to its fullest extent because you're afraid of saying the wrong thing.

- You don't engage with the world and take up space because you don't have the ideal skin, the ideal weight, the ideal... (fill in the blank).

when you embrace perfectionism, you abandon yourself

- You deny your worth because you're not at the level that you yourself have deemed worthy.

- You unwittingly uphold systems of oppression because that's the "natural order" of things and perfection doesn't allow for disruption.

- By rejecting your perceived flaws, you make it less likely that other people around you will accept theirs.

curiosity, innovation

and liberation

The alternative is to accept that you are human and will inevitably get things wrong. Yes, it will be uncomfortable. Yes, you'll let people down. And yes, you'll have to apologize for your mistakes. But on the other side of that is curiosity, innovation and ultimately liberation from a system that was always designed to keep you down.

THE -ISMS

For some of us, resilience involves having to exist within systems that were literally designed with our oppression in mind. The -isms, including racism, sexism, heterosexism and ableism contribute to burnout in different ways as they all create chronic stress in those that they target.

- **Racism:** racism (or any -ism) doesn't have to be experienced directly to have damaging effects. Stress can surge simply after hearing about other people from your identity group being discriminated against or as a result of remembering/anticipating experiences when you are marginalized yourself.

Racism is significantly associated with poorer physical and mental health. Resulting conditions include diabetes, obesity, depression, anxiety, suicidal behaviour and post-traumatic stress disorder (PTSD).

- **Sexism:** Both overt and covert sexism are just as detrimental to an employee's well-being at work as other job stressors including inter-role conflict, role ambiguity and job overload.

Perceived sexism has been linked to depression, psychological distress, high blood pressure, greater premenstrual symptoms, nausea and headaches. Experiencing sexism is also correlated to an increase in stress hormones.

- **Heterosexism:** Heterosexism includes the victimization, homophobia, discrimination, self-stigma and sexual identity concealment that gay, lesbian, bisexual, queer and transgender people experience.

A 2015 study carried out on mental health professionals (MHP) found that sexual-minority-identified MHPs report higher rates of burnout when compared to heterosexual-identified MHPs.

Contributing factors include perceptions of workplace heterosexism, perceptions of workplace support and identity concealment.

- **Ableism:** Ableism includes discrimination and social prejudice against people with disabilities or who are perceived to have disabilities.

Those who choose to hide their disabilities often live in fear of being discovered and work harder to compensate for any perceived difference. Others may find themselves trapped in jobs where they don't feel appreciated, lack learning opportunities and potential for advancement.

self-compassion stems from a desire to be kind to yourself when things are going badly

self-compassion

Self-compassion means a willingness to be kind to yourself in times of suffering. Rather than affirm that "all is well", it helps you to get in touch with how you're really feeling and gives you a space to be vulnerable with the pain. It consists of three separate components:

Mindfulness: Bringing awareness to how you are feeling.

Common humanity: Linking your experience to the human experience.

Kindness: Offering yourself words and actions that express loving care.

Unlike self-esteem, self-compassion stems from a desire to be kind to yourself when things are going badly, as opposed to the pride you take in yourself when doing something well. It helps you to accept yourself as a human being who, despite being very capable of making mistakes, deserves to be treated with kindness and respect. Always.

SELF-COMPASSION BREAK

A self-compassion break was developed by Dr Kristin Neff and combines the three elements of self-compassion in an easy way that you can do at any moment throughout the day. It acknowledges that you are in a moment of suffering, that suffering is part of life and that you wish to be kind to yourself. Follow the steps below:

1   Take a few deep belly breaths to settle your mind. Place both hands, one on top of the other, over the centre of your heart. This is a gesture of self-acceptance.

2   Now say the following:
"This is really difficult."
"Difficult moments like these are part of life."
"Even when it's hard, may I treat myself with kindness. May I give myself the love that I need."

3   Finish with a few more deep breaths and let the moment pass.

kindness in action

Self-compassion isn't just what you say, but also what you do. Through your actions, you affirm that even in times of difficulty, you're going to be loyal to yourself. Some ways to be kind to yourself include:

- **Taking a sip of water and pairing it with an affirmation (e.g. "Because I'm worth it")**

- **Going outside for a walk and connecting with nature**

- **Buying yourself flowers (a personal favourite)**

- **Preparing a meal with fresh, vibrant foods for yourself**

- **Drawing yourself a warm bath**

- **Taking a dance break**

- **Turning your phone off early and disconnecting for a night**

- **Giving yourself a massage with your favourite body oil.**

where are you feeling tense?

LET'S GET COMFORTABLE

So many of my clients who are on the brink of burnout or in the early stages of recovery don't give much thought to their own comfort. Skipping meals, holding pee, skimping on sleep, resisting rest ... basic needs go unmet all day long. Are you ready to get comfortable? Here are a few questions to help get you started:

1   **How are you sitting?** Could you use an extra cushion, maybe a different chair?

2   **How are you breathing?** Can you take the next minute to breathe a little deeper?

3   **Are you warm enough?** Could you use an extra blanket or a pair of fuzzy slippers?

4   **Are you thirsty?** Does your mouth feel parched? When was the last time you drank a glass of water?

5   **Where are you feeling tense?** Roll your head from side to side, stretch your arms above your head, shake your body and let the stress fall away.

Ironically, making yourself comfortable can be out of your comfort zone, especially if you're used to withholding things until you feel you've earned it. What's your relationship with comfort? How can you make yourself more comfortable today?

gratitude

When it comes to mastering stress and building resilience against burnout, gratitude is non-negotiable. Choosing to cultivate an attitude of gratitude will improve both your physical and psychological health. They've actually found that grateful people experience fewer aches and pains and find it easier to sleep at night. On the emotional front, gratitude helps reduce feelings of envy, resentment, frustration and regret. It also enhances empathy, allowing us to be more sensitive towards others and therefore less likely to act aggressively or seek revenge. As if those benefits weren't enough, gratitude also improves self-esteem. It has been found that people who practice gratitude regularly tend to compare themselves less to other people. Instead, they're able to appreciate others' accomplishments and wish them well. If you've ever found yourself with a bad case of comparisonitis, you'll want to take a minute and shine a light on all of the good things that you have to be grateful for in your own life.

There are so many ways to practice gratitude, but this technique will help you gain greater appreciation for three areas of your life that you can so easily take for granted:

1 Set aside about ten minutes at the end of the day. You can even keep a notepad by your bedside to write on just before you go to sleep.

2 Write down five to ten things that you're grateful for in the following categories:

- Body

Example: I'm grateful that I can walk, talk, chew my food, breathe without assistance.

- Relationships

Example: I'm grateful for my partner and the text message he sent to cheer me up, my parents and their health, my son and all of his hugs.

- Material possessions

Example: I'm grateful for my apartment, my laptop, my phone and my books.

3 Repeat this practice every day for a week and notice how your gratitude and appreciation for life starts to grow.

QUESTIONS FOR REFLECTION

1 In what areas of your life have you adopted a
   fixed mindset? What would change for you if you
   released the idea that you "had to make it work"
   and every mistake was a personal failing?

....
....
....

2 What role does perfectionism currently play in your
   life? How does it affect your current levels of stress?

....
....
....

3 What kind words do you say to other people when
   they are suffering? What would it be like to say
   these to yourself?

....
....
....

4 What four feelings would you like to experience on
   a more regular basis? Use them to create your own
   self-compassion affirmation.

....
....
....

what role does perfectionism currently play in your life?

boundaries

9

"No is a complete sentence."

"Is that what you said to her?"

"I sure did, Jolinda. First, I told her 'no' and when she asked me why, I looked her straight in the eyes and said, 'I don't need to explain my reasons. No is a complete sentence.'"

My client Serena had been working on prioritizing her needs in both her personal and professional life for the last three months. She had come to our session that day with a story about a co-worker who wanted to add yet another huge responsibility to her already-full workload. Although she knew what a positive difference her participation would make, she also recognized that she was already at capacity and was under no obligation to be the saviour in this situation.

When we started working together, Serena said that saying no was one of the hardest things for her to do. As a licensed social worker, being a nurturer came naturally to her. Whenever someone was in need, she was always there to jump in and offer help. As the director of a mental health clinic where she had worked for over 20 years, she felt comfortable being the leader and people always looked to her for guidance when challenges arose. She had given her energy and time away so frequently, however, that she had very little of either left for herself.

no is a complete sentence

Tired of being so tired, we identified areas where Serena could start bringing her life back into balance. After our initial conversation it became clear that boundaries were sorely lacking and that creating them together would be the most logical place to start. By the end of her six-month series, she had discovered the joy that comes with valuing her needs and being loyal to herself no matter what. That's what boundaries are all about.

the power of no

It's such a simple word, isn't it? And yet so many of us have a hard time saying it.

Do you have a minute? Sure (when you really don't).

Do you mind doing me a favour? Of course (when you actually need help yourself).

Could we meet on Tuesday instead of Wednesday? No problem (even though it means missing out on something you wanted to do for yourself).

Can we meet at my place? Yep (despite the fact that you always go to their place and they never come to yours).

Shall we split a bottle? Sounds good (when you would prefer to drink water instead of wine).

In each of the above examples, saying yes means denying your own wants and needs. You might not be saying no to other people, but you're certainly saying no to yourself. If you're anything like my clients, you probably struggle with putting yourself first. Like me, you might have been raised in a household where being selfish was something to be avoided and being selfless was a quality to be revered. Putting yourself last, however, is bad news when it comes to building resilience against chronic stress and burnout. Can you identify with any of these situations?

- You never have enough time to devote to projects and activities that bring you joy.

- You feel overwhelmed by the social commitments that flood your calendar.

- You don't get enough sleep because you stay up late to get everything done.

- You're exhausted from taking on responsibilities that aren't even yours.

- You feel angry and resentful because you're constantly giving away your most valuable time.

Saying no is often uncomfortable, but indeed

necessary for achieving the happiness and fulfilment that you deserve. It involves putting limits on your time, being fiercely committed to your own self-care and giving yourself permission to fill your own cup. But before you can do any of that, you must first acknowledge that you're worth it.

self-worth

All boundary work starts with self-worth. Unlike self-esteem, which is highly dependent on your evaluation of yourself in comparison to others and highly variable depending on the feelings you have towards your accomplishments, self-worth is inviolable and never-changing. Despite the messages you may have received around your worth being tied to your productivity or your ability to carry out your assigned tasks, it really is something that remains with you until the day you die. Simply by being here and being human, you are worthy.

Think of a time when you wanted to say no to someone, but instead you said yes. Now ask yourself if your decision would have been different had you believed that your needs and desires were just as important as the person you agreed to do something for. See if you can identify the fear that was holding you back. For some of us it's the fear of rejection, for others it's the fear of anger, or it could be the fear of disappointing them. Continue reflecting on this situation and see if you can remember how your body responded. Was there a feeling of tension or ease, restriction or expansion? What would have been the worst-case scenario, had you trusted your inner wisdom and said no instead?

Many of my clients struggle with decisions that have the potential for causing other people pain, even if they're the ones who are suffering the most. You could be more willing to break your own heart if what you really want has the potential to cause someone else harm. Sometimes you have to be the villain in someone else's story to be the hero in your own. Even when the boundaries you set for yourself aren't well received, you are always worthy of protecting your needs.

while all boundaries are essentially about protecting your needs, there are actually a number of different types

TYPES OF BOUNDARIES

While all boundaries are essentially about protecting your needs, there are actually a number of different types:

- **Physical:** Physical boundaries have to do with your personal space and your physical body.

- **Emotional**: Emotional boundaries have to do with recognizing your feelings and identifying which ones are unique to you, independent of the feelings of others.

- **Mental:** Mental boundaries have to do with how comfortable you are with expressing your thoughts and listening to those of other people.

- **Time:** Time boundaries have to do with your willingness to spend your time as you see fit, dedicating it to the people and activities that are most important to you.

- **Material:** Material boundaries have to do with your personal belongings, including money, and who you share them with

- **Sexual:** Sexual boundaries have to do with who you consent to have sex with, what the parameters are for safe sex and what feels pleasurable to you.

the boundaries you set with yourself

When considering boundaries and choosing those that will make the biggest difference to your physical and emotional well-being, don't forget those that you also have to set with yourself. Setting these kinds of boundaries is especially important when starting a new habit or breaking an old pattern. At some point, it will be necessary to say no to one thing and yes to another. For example:

- When you decide you no longer want to stay up past 10 p.m.

- When you decide you no longer want to snack mindlessly in front of the TV.

- When you decide you no longer want to skip your morning workout in favour of sleeping in.

Setting your own boundaries can feel a lot like being your own parent since they often have to do with creating structure and routine. It doesn't always feel good to set these kinds of limits, but in your heart of hearts you know that it will do you a world of good. If you struggle with this, try pairing your new boundary with some kind of reward. For example, if you no longer want to stay up late, make your bedroom a

being your own parent

truly inviting place. You might like to invest in high-quality bedding and luxurious pyjama sets. If you no longer want to snack mindlessly in front of the TV, prepare yourself a nightly cup of tea. Turn it into a ritual with a special pot and a beautiful cup or mug. If you no longer want to hit the snooze button and would like to get your morning workout in, find a playlist that gets you going and workout clothes that you actually enjoy wearing.

The boundary that I have the hardest time enforcing on myself is going to bed on time. As I mentioned in an earlier chapter, I've always loved staying up late,

pair your boundary

with a reward

but I also know the damage this does to my body. While I don't have to be asleep as early as my son suggests, it certainly doesn't hurt to start winding down after tucking him in. Saying yes to an earlier bedtime means saying no to social media scrolling, no to series binge watching and no to late-night conversations with clients, family and friends. It's not always easy, but doing so allows me to wake up with the energy I need to be at my best the following day.

BOUNDARIES IN ACTION

Below, you'll find examples of what each type of boundary might look like when enforced in real life, both with other people and with yourself.

PHYSICAL:

- **Others:** Refuse to invite people into your space if you don't actually want them there.

- **Self:** Have a dedicated space for working and another for eating.

EMOTIONAL:

- **Others:** Hold space for other people without taking on their feelings about a situation.

- **Self:** Acknowledge your feelings through journaling and regularly checking in with your body.

MENTAL:

- **Others:** Have the courage to express your opinion, even when it's different from somebody else's.

- **Self:** Be honest with yourself when you don't know something and be willing to learn.

TIME:

- **Others:** Turn down invitations if you would rather have time for yourself.

- **Self:** Go to bed at a consistent time every day, including weekends.

MATERIAL:

- **Others:** Only lend your belongings to people you know will take good care of them.

- **Self:** Buy things that you know you'll use and truly appreciate.

SEXUAL:

- **Others:** Consent to sex or any other intimate activity when it feels right for you.

- **Self:** Trust your decision to wait if your body is saying no.

set, enforce, model

If you're new to setting boundaries, it can feel like a courageous act to say no for the first time. You might encounter people who aren't used to hearing it or, when they do, they take it as a challenge. Unfortunately, saying no once is rarely enough.
If you want to set boundaries that people actually respect, you must:

1 **Set the boundary**

2 **Enforce the boundary**

3 **Model the boundary**

When you set the boundary, you are making it clear to the other person what you are no longer willing to tolerate. As my client Serena says, no is indeed a complete sentence, but it could also sound like:

- **I'm not interested in doing that (anymore).**

- **It really makes me feel uncomfortable when ...**

- **That doesn't work for me.**

- **Please stop.**

enforce
the
boundary

When you enforce the boundary, you're essentially reminding the other person of the previous agreement. If someone benefited from your lack of boundaries in the past, it's likely that they'll challenge them going forward. Always remember that you're allowed to want what you want, even when they try to convince you otherwise. Enforcing boundaries can sound like:

- My decision still stands. Nothing's changed on my end.

- I understand that you would like me to come, but I still won't be able to.

- As I've mentioned before, I don't mind if you drink, but I feel a lot better if I don't. Please stop asking me.

- Remember when I said no the other day? I feel the same way now.

When you model the boundary, you're remaining steadfast in your decision and consistent in your behaviour. If you want people to believe that no means no, you have to show them through your actions. That's not to say that your boundaries have to be the same with every individual across the board, but if you say that you won't tolerate something from one person, it can help if they see you following the standard you've set in other situations as well.

you're allowed to want what you want

Healthy relationships, both in your personal and professional life, not only require boundaries, but also the kind of open and honest communication that helps establish them. If you don't feel safe enough to share your boundary, it's possible that you're in a relationship that doesn't have your best interests at heart. While the decision to leave may feel like an impossible option, or perhaps the last resort, remaining in a situation lacking in mutual respect will create its own kind of stress. Trusting yourself enough to go with your gut and defend your needs might not be easy, but denying your truth isn't a good alternative either. Sometimes you have to choose your hand.

when was the last time you said no to someone?

QUESTIONS FOR REFLECTION

1 Which types of boundaries are easiest for you to set? Which are the most difficult?

....

....

2 When was the last time you said no to someone? What was that experience like for you? How did it feel? What were the consequences?

....

....

3 What's one boundary you would like to set with someone else in the next 30 days? What's one boundary you would like to set with yourself?

....

....

4 Imagine you are a person who always puts themselves first. What would your relationship with boundaries be like? How would this change things for you?

....

....

are
you
ready?

10

Over the last few years, I've realized that a huge part of my calling is helping people experience vibrant health so they can become more resilient against burnout and fulfil their unique missions in the world. This is why I get out of bed every morning, why I share my story, why I keep going when the going gets tough (and quite frankly, as a single mother in a foreign country battling two invisible illnesses, it's not always easy). But that's what a calling requires – resilience, persistence and grit.

I know what it's like to feel disempowered by medical professionals, to go through health challenges without support, to feel like your body is betraying you, to feel like you just want to quit on yourself because you've tried it all with no results. But I also know what it feels like to heal, to nourish my body with what it really needs, to have the time and space to hear my own voice and move past deeply ingrained wounds. I know what it feels like to be honoured for the woman that I am, in my queerness, in my humanness and to feel connected to something much larger than myself along the way.

If you want to make that giant leap towards the life of your dreams, you'll need your physical health, your hormonal health, your mental health and your spiritual health on your side. You can eat all the right foods and do all the right exercises, buy organic this and non-toxic that, but if your spirit is broken and you're doing those things from a place of fear, need for control or a lack of trust in your intuition and what your body knows is best, you'll never experience genuine well-being.

When I was diagnosed with my autoimmune disease 12 years ago, I was a vegan studying holistic nutrition and knew everyone at my organic food market by name. I was also in chronic pain and unable to walk down the street most days without wincing. Two things had to happen before I started feeling better: 1) I had to start eating according to what my body actually needed and 2) take a cold, hard look at what in my life was no longer serving me.

I had a more or less easy time modifying my diet, but it was the life stuff that was the hardest. I was in a relationship that I knew wasn't good for me, but hey, at least I had someone. I was in a job that I dreaded going to every day, but hey, at least I was employed. I had turned my back on all of the spiritual teachings I had grown up with as a child, but hey, what difference would believing in something greater than myself make anyway? (Spoiler alert: all the difference.) Since then, I've changed a lot. I've come home to myself. I began to work towards what I really wanted and how I truly desired to live. Now I know how to take care of myself, to honour my inner wisdom and surrender to the flow of life.

If it wasn't for my own coaches, healers and spiritual teachers supporting me during those times when I didn't want to take the difficult path, I would probably still be stuck. Stuck doing "all the things, all the time", still feeling miserable, still cycling through the phases of burnout. Within the pages of this book, I've done my best to give you practical ideas and tangible steps that you can easily implement into your life. It's my hope that you'll put what you've learned into action and will become more resilient against the effects of chronic stress as a result.

Stress is inevitable. Burnout is optional. Resilience is possible. Are you ready?

stress is
inevitable.
burnout is
optional.
resilience
is possible.
are you
ready?

Jolinda Johnson is an award-winning Certified Life Coach, Holistic Health Coach, and Priestess for feminists, BIPOC, and LGBTQIA+ folx. She is a burnout specialist, using a hybrid of holistic health and life coaching paired with scientific education to help people manage stress and build resilience. This is her first book.

FURTHER READING

The Adrenal-Thyroid Revolution, Aviva Romm, MD

Atomic Habits, James Clear

Brilliant Burnout, Nisha Jackson, PhD

Burnout, Emily Nagoski PhD and Amelia Nagoski, DMA

The Compassionate Mind, Paul Gilbert

The Hormone Cure, Sara Gottfried, MD

The Mindful Way Through Depression, Mark Williams, John Teasdale, Zindel Segal, Jon Kabat-Zinn

Neurofitness, Rahul Jandial, MD, PhD

Sacred Rest, Saundra Dalton-Smith, MD

Self-Compassion, Kristin Neff, PhD

The Self-Worth Safari, John Niland

Set Boundaries, Find Peace, Nedra Glover Tawwab

Setting Boundaries Will Set You Free, Nancy Levin

Widen the Window, Elizabeth A. Stanley, PhD

Why We Sleep, Matthew Walker